ASHES

by

DAVID RUDKIN

SAMUEL FRENCH

LONDON

NEW YORK   TORONTO   SYDNEY   HOLLYWOOD

CAST OF CHARACTERS

ASHES was given its premiere at the Open Space Theatre, London on January 9th, 1974, with the following cast:

Colin	Peter McEnery
Anne	Lynn Farleigh
Doctor/Surgeon/Guru	Ian Collier
Jennifer/Receptionist/Valerie	Penny Ryder

Directed by Pam Brighton

Designed by William Dudley

CHARACTERS

COLIN, early thirties, Northern Irish, was a writer, now a teacher

ANNE, late twenties, his wife, West Riding, was an actress, now a teacher

An averagely presentable couple, neither sexually glamorous nor pathetically unprepossessing. COLIN cared more how he dressed five years ago: a good pair of unflared corduroys he wore for best then he uses at work today; plain shirt, tie, quilted anorak, hush puppies. ANNE had more style, but now they live far from shops and have less money—a neutral grey smock, fashionable once, now she knocks about in.

Other Characters

DOCTOR

SEMINOLOGIST ("GURU")

GYNAECOLOGICAL SURGEON

AMBULANCE DRIVER

AREA ADOPTIONS OFFICER

JENNIFER, medical student

RECEPTIONIST at Guru's

VALERIE, fecund neighbour

NURSE

MRS JONES, assistant Adoptions Officer

These rôles should be taken by one male and one female actor; but in this doubling there is no thematic significance. To cast each separately is possible, but would tell, I think, against the 'minimal' method of the play.

STAGING

A small auditorium is preferable. No set as such is called for: a manoeuvrable rostrum (for bed, couch, etc.); plain upright chairs; a doctor's desk (perhaps, for variety, two—one L, one R). On a very small stage, white screens or traverse curtains can be used to mask, discover, suggest change of location, etc. (as in the Open Space production, to great effect). On a larger stage, these effects should be sought with light.

The clinical processes shown should be at root authentic, but reduced to a spare theatrical severity. As to the indignities to which Colin and Anne submit themselves, they must not make light of them, nor ever cheaply clown them; rather, bring us into a wry factual sharing of them. They may, of course, tempt us here and there into a tasteless or ignorant laugh: where so, with the line that follows, or by their stillness, deliver any necessary rebuke.

The play's running-time has ranged from a hundred minutes to two-and-a-quarter hours. This is not a question so much of whether a production is a fast or a slow one; it depends also, of course, on how much, if at all, the audience laugh during the opening scenes, where most of the play's humour is concentrated: but another factor, to which this play is uniquely susceptible, is the size of the auditorium. If the actors have to project this text, in order to bring the audience in to something which is essentially intimate, they have to do so with especial subtlety: and this, in performance, can take time. In any case, for the sake of the play's three-movement form, it should be given **without interval**. In the Young Vic production a break was made, after Colin's "extinction" speech on page 38; at Los Angeles, after Anne's "Mozart, Darwin" speech on page 31. I do not endorse either procedure.

I

Darkness. From speakers round auditorium a man's deep rhythmic breathing subsides toward silence. Suddenly, from behind a screen or from slow stage-gloom, the thrash and sense of a brief bedtussle—

Colin   (*unseen there. Yelp of trivial pain. Voice barely recognizable as Northern Irish: characteristic ou- and r-sounds, hint of Antrim tune*) Ow no—do you have to do that now?

Anne   (*unseen there. Quiet voice, just recognizable as West Riding: trace of back a-sound, tune*) When else do I get? Never still enough.

Colin   Gouging.

Anne   Not gouging.

Colin   Each twinge runs to the knackers like some Turkish torture.

Anne   (*mocking*) Poor knackers . . .

Colin   Leave over!

Anne   I've nearly got it . . .

Colin   (*threat*) I'll pull him out—

Anne   There. A lovely huge one, juicy and black. What was so bad about that?

Colin   How do you tell in the dark what colour?

Anne   I've had me eye on that since before we put the lights out.

Colin   Preying mantis 'll never be extinct while you're alive.

Anne   The human skin must breathe.

Colin   You've not been aroused by me at all—

Anne   Don't be fatuous—

Colin   All my foreplay reefed on your single expectation of winkling out one clotted pore.

Anne   I like my man to be healthy.

Colin   Post-coital triumph more like. Penis jealousy.

Anne   What? Flatter yourself.

Colin   (*pause*) I never had blackheads till you started purging them.

Anne   Not true. (*pause*) None of your other bedmates bothered, you mean. Whatever sex they were.

Colin   They: weren't cannibals.

Anne   (*pausing*) Getting heavy, love.

Colin   (*put out*) Sorry.

Anne   (*pause; quieter*) Mop up now.

Colin	Ay. Load delivered, back to yard. (*If house laugh, cut following:*) Cold half of bed.

They have separated. Long pause.

Anne	Perhaps we did it this time.

Snap up stagelight. Colin remains, unpresent, Anne's half of bed is now a doctor's couch: on which Anne lies supine, head toward us, bare legs raised in a coital posture. Doctor—freshfaced, early thirties, slight hint of the farmer—gently, firmly, palps her belly to feel that everything is in its proper place.

Doctor	(*faintest last trace of rural speech; frank, unpatronizing*) How long have you and your husband been trying for a conception, Mrs Harding?
Anne	Two years.
Doctor	Then you *do* have a problem. Forgive me: you are doing it right?
Anne	Do we look fools?
Doctor	I've had couples trying to conceive through the navel. (*He manipulates, palps*) No sign of damage or deformity, no displacement . . . Very nice set of organs, Mrs Harding; compact . . . Your husband is potent, you say; your blood-groups compatible; your cycle short and regular—
Anne	(*bitter*) Clockwork.
Doctor	Which I like. Well. First I think we should take a PC sample—
Anne	Post-coital—
Doctor	(*surprised she knows*) Have you been a nurse?
Anne	No.
Doctor	(*pause; comes away, peels off a disposable glove into wastebasket*) Well you can probably work out for yourself what a post-coital test involves. Round about the tenth or eleventh day of your next cycle—

Cut light. In darkness, loud alarmclock. From Colin and Anne there, soon sounds of waking, shifting. Cut alarm.

Anne	(*yawning, unseen there*) God, what an hour. Why so early?
Colin	(*yawning, unseen there*) Specimen, love.
Anne	Mm?
Colin	Specimen. We have to provide a characteristic sample of our mixture. Fresh.
Anne	(*miserable, tired*) Oh fuck—
Colin	Something like that.
Anne	I'll have to have a pee.

Anne heard stumbling away off:

Put 'fire on, love.

Colin   *(grumbling, moving)* Mouth like a bloody parrotcage . . .

> *Slow, dim glow as of electric barfire: form of Colin crouching before it. Loud on speakers: urine trickling into water; rip, scuff of tissue paper; chain pulled.*

Romantic.

Anne   *(dim shape returns there, shuddering)* Right then. Man. I'm all cold and pissy for you : come and give. *(Lies, head toward us, raising opened legs—)*

> *Up stagelight. Jennifer, student in white coat, assists objectively throughout. Doctor standing bowed with some unseen medical implement inserted between Anne's raised legs. A careful snipping sound, then Doctor draws implement out, away. Jennifer helps Doctor transfer smear to a slide. Doctor peels off disposable glove into waste-basket; Jennifer brings slide, sets it in microscope. Doctor comes, peers into microscope. Anne meanwhile relaxes up into sitting pose on bed's side, watches in anxiety:*

Doctor   *(at last)* Jennifer. *(very quiet)*

Jennifer   Doctor?

Doctor   *(very quiet)* These sperms are all dead, wouldn't you say?

Jennifer   *(looks)* Oh no, Doctor, I think there's one.

Doctor   One what?

Jennifer   One sperm alive.

Doctor   Where? *(looks)* Where?

Jennifer   Five o'clock.

Doctor   *(seems at last to find it)* Oh yes. Oh no. Oh no, Jennifer, that's a blemish in the slide. *(quieter)* Appointment to see the husband, I think.

> *Lightchange: Colin emerging into presence, his side of the bed, trousers and briefs down. Doctor disposes of smeared slide into waste-tin, draws on another glove, goes up to Colin. Colin stands, to have his genitals examined. Doctor partmasks him, professionally observing a patient's privacy.*

Colin   The self-consciousness of the situation has shrunk him rather.

Doctor   *(droll)* Testicles, not the penis, deliver the goods. *(To check that testicles are free:)* Cough please.

> *Colin coughs.*

Again.

> *Colin coughs.*

No injury at any time?

Colin None.

Doctor No growth, clotting . . .?

Colin That I know of . . .

Doctor No reason why normal testicles should not produce good semen. Yet you know by the time yours gets where it matters your semen is useless. I shall give you a letter—

> *Lightchange, Doctor going. Colin emerges, pulling up briefs, trousers. While as yet keeping us at some distance, he puts on an act for us:*

Colin *(imitates a woman receptionist)* "Yes sir, can I help you?" *(self)* I have this letter. It is about a sperm count. *(woman)* "Oh, this is Family Planning. You want Fertility. Up the stairs, sir."

> *His trousers are up now. He looks at us, making us feel a little easier in his company. Now he goes into another act, a vocal send-up of a Brummy lab assistant:*

"Here y'are then, friend: a room apart. Produce your sample, bring it back to the lab when yow've done. We send yow the bill for two smacker, yowr doctor the result in twenty-one days. Venetian blind don't work, I'm sorry to say, but nobody to overlook yow. Lock on the door don't work either, I'm sorry to say, but they all know here what this room is for. *(confidential)* Some blokes has to get their wives to help them wi this at home, then bring the product in to us by buz. Take your time."

> *Colin is staring us out again: his expression never breaks, yet somehow he is charming us into a humorous sharing of his absurd predicament. Yet nothing must rupture his essential privateness. Fade up shouts, whistlings, sounds of buildingsite outside, above; Colin glances up, out toward these once or twice. He takes out of his pocket a tiny glass or plastic container—two inches deep at most, neck barely an inch across, with blank label. He looks up from this to us. The buildingsite sounds worry him. And an anatomical problem: how to address an erection to this ludicrous jar? With simple precise gestures he sketches one or two ways that occur to him. Impossible. A third way. Even more absurd. He catches our eye, goes to sit on chair near curtain, plays for time. Has thought: takes out pencil-stub, writes on label. Shows us:*

My name. Against confusion.

Sits, drums fingers. Another idea: puts jar on floor, all but gets down on to all fours above it—A builder's voice calling someone above outside— Colin sharp back on his chair again, jar in hand.

Crossfade in clinic sounds: trolleys in corridors, someone on intercom calling for a doctor. After a moment Colin sees he must make a real effort. He brings chair down, drops trousers, turns back on us:

(over shoulder to us) What are yous expectin to see, then?

Sits. Makes discreetest gesture of fondling; soon perhaps, a little tsk-tsk sound as though geeing-up a diminutive horse between his thighs there. Soon.

(gentle) There's a fella. There's a fella.

Sound of door opened, shriek of young girl—Colin sharply rises, hands covering himself. Clattering heels flee, a stifled giggle; giggles shared afar.

(over shoulder to us) Was ever fella so abused?

Crossfade in buildingsite sounds, jolly whistlings, etc. An idea:

(to penis) We'll go an shufty at the builder boys. There's maybe a nice arse'll turn ye on.

Part-hauling trousers up, makes off above—suddenly comes hurrying back for jar. Off again. Cut sounds. Lightchange. From where Colin went now Doctor comes, labelled jar in hand, now containing a milky dreg. Goes to sit behind desk:

Doctor   Colin Harding, his seed. There's life in this, the clinic tell me: though not so much as I should like.

Colin, dressed again, comes bringing chair, to sit before desk.

You could conceive with this semen, Mr Harding; but it would be a miracle.

Colin   *(no aggression; acceptance merely)* You mean my seed is sterile?

Doctor   No. A hundred or so million sperms per millilitre a man ejaculates when making love: only one of these need reach the ovum, to conceive. But all x hundred million need to be very lively, for there to be that chance.

Colin   Mine are not—lively.

Doctor	Too few of them are. They litter this fluid like so many stunned tadpoles, I'm afraid.
Colin	*(pause)* Can anything be done. *(NB almost no question tone)*
Doctor	You can help. Use a shower from now, not a bath. Scrap your tight briefs for boxer-shorts. It takes six weeks to make a sperm, and requires a temperature in the scrotum two degrees lower than that of the body. Which is why in hot weather, you will have noticed, your ballocks dangle. Circulation. So, every morning and every evening for the next six weeks, bathe your testicles in the coldest water, several minutes at a time. At the end of January, go back for another sperm count. Central heating, you know, probably reduces male fertility more than any other factor in the West. I think also you should eat less: hunger helps fecundity.

> *Doctor disposes (discreetly, but the moment is not lost on us) of Colin's semen-specimen into wastebasket; goes. Lightchange.*

| Colin | *(to us)* Hands up who's tried bathing his balls. Dangle them in a bowl, do I hear ye say? Some anatomy: you try that. *(A minimal sufficient mime)* A flannel, then? Not very effective. Stand akimbo in the bath, a cold shower aimed upwards? *(Mimes this. Mimes getting soaked)* One foot outside the bath, then, the other across? *(Mimes this, chair as bath)* Marginally improved for access: if you don't mind cleaning the floor down twice a day. I doubt even a bidet's not much help, in my precise predicament. But, for those of you, for those of you who may at some time need it, a solution does emerge. Sit back on the bog pan, your legs priapically wide; grip the showerhead in one hand, in the other exposing the scrotum to its full freezing blast. December. Friends in the house over Christmas— *(Birmingham speech)* "Mom, what's that funny splashing in the bathroom?" The things a silly sod'll do for fatherhood. Or is it fatherhood? Might it not rather be, for the myth of "manliness"? |

> *Stands; turns up, speaks as to someone in a new scene:*

Hello, I'm back again.

> *Almost a one-man crosstalk act for us, with Brummy lab assistant:*

"Six weeks on the cold water then, have you, friend? Mind you, can work a charm. In you get, then: wanker's paradise. Not my idea of one, though. Still: they find it easier the second time." *(Self, dry)* Ay. I thought to pick up this time a certain class of picture-book. *(Lab assistant)* "Visual aid?"

(Self) An honest usage, Longford missed. *(Away off, factually letting us glimpse two "cake" magazines he has: one of women, one of young men)*

Anne comes down, with letters.

Anne   Enter wife, reading aloud for audience's benefit several convenient letters. Marj is expecting. Valerie is expecting. Cynthia's in pod again. None of them planned for. Wendy miscounts on the pill; Hilary's Albert comes home from a police course randy as hell, no time for precautions, wham bam thank you, ma'am, hey-ho another bottle shot from the shelf. Click from a man's pants, some women. *(Last letter)* From the doctor. Sperm motility now normal, quote: if you go overdue, inform me. After three or four months I do. First time in my bleeding life, overdue. I say No, it's a freak. Or hysterical. Twenty-nine days, for me unheard of. Thirty. He's telling himself Stop thinking about it, stop hoping: watched pot and that. We've clicked or we haven't. Thirty-one days. If we can hang on till only Monday, hang out the flags, I'm qualifying for a Urine Test! Thirty-two days. Every time I'm out of the room now, I can hear his ears pricked for the sound of the door of the cupboard where I keep my pads. Thirty-third day. No gutrot. No pain in the back, no heaviness in the breasts. Just the blood. *(Pause. Sits)*

Colin comes quietly.

Colin   Bad one?

He doesn't need telling. He reaches, touches her: but there is nothing in the touch; in the tenderness is something hard, hurt. Anne turns her head from him, moves her Colinward hand across herself from him: remains so, frozen, unpresent.

Enter Guru: greying, short hair, fine-rimmed spectacles, Edinburgh accent of professional class.

Guru   *(to us)* I am an expensive seminologist. My two new patients dub me the Guru because they get the impression I think I am omniscient. Indeed, I do occasionally speak as though I personally had invented the first idea of everything, including coitus itself. *(Sits behind desk)*

Guru's lady Receptionist, impeccably manicured, the type to make a man feel he reeks of sweat, comes for Colin.

Receptionist   Mr Harding?

Colin   *(follows her)* Colin Harding yes, I have an appointment—Dr Mc . . .

Receptionist   I'm sure your accent will make Dr McAnespie feel quite at
               home. What part of Scotland are you from?

Colin   County Antrim.

Receptionist   *(pause)* Not a very happy place, these days.

               Colin can say nothing to that. Receptionist leaves
               him seated opposite Guru; Anne, screenmasked, or,
               if no screens, unpresent. Guru now has file of letters
               on desk before him.

Colin   Doctor, I am not a superstitious man. Forgive me if this
               question sounds benighted. My very first erotic urges—the
               earliest I remember—were to bite lumps out of classmates'
               buttocks in the showers: especially the hairier ones, as I
               myself was never very hairily endowed. I'm still tormented
               with a ravening homosexual self.

Guru   *(gentle)* Oh, there is no such thing as a "homosexual self".
               Sexuality runs deeper than culture, how can it discriminate;
               why should it, as culture does? You have a sexual self. That
               is your central essential energy, deeper, truer than any cul-
               tural self: homo- and hetero- are straws on the surface. A
               single-sex school you were at?

Colin   Oh, a day one, but very ancient:* the usual seedbed of gentle
               Christian fascism. The cult of the Chap, the heroic unattain-
               able ideal: from which régime an inadequate like me is
               expected at nineteen miraculously to blossom straight. Ten
               years of my adult emotional life that schooling cost me, ten
               maimed years: I know where I would put a bomb if a
               Fenian ever gave me one. No child of mine must ever go to
               such a place. I fought hard—not to convert my sexuality
               from one orientation to another, but to broaden it to include
               the opposite sex as well. I refused to be the stunted end of a
               tree. A hard fight; I have won. My sexual world is very dis-
               cordant now, but for all the vain yearning my several lusts
               put me in, I am glad in their diversity and would not be
               without one of them. Out from this all, my wife is the best
               thing has happened me. Now we want children. For years
               we have had no luck, and it is inexplicable—you have the
               history of it there. So I ask this. It will sound naïve, but this is
               now something of a mortal strait for me, and when our back
               is to the wall we think irrational things: can there be, can
               there be at all any connection, any causality, between the
               homo-erotics I still also so strongly feel, and the dying of my
               seed?

* For the Dublin production—where the audience would have taken this as a reference to a
Catholic (e.g. Christian Brothers') school—I added here "of Tudor foundation". Where
such confusion is possible, Colin should probably (outside Ireland) amplify instead with
"of Anglican foundation".

Guru	If you believe in a crabbèd heterosexual fatherGod, you could call your plight a Judgement. If you believe what you are paying me seven old guineas for, then I, as a man of reason and acquainted with chemistry, say No cause, no cause. Just stretch the skin tighter over your testicles when you bathe them; and two minutes only, twice in the day. Continue the cold water, until you have conceived.
Colin	But could worry, or stress of any kind . . . ? Or if my work were not going well, or if I were at some professional crisis . . . ?

> *Guru checks through letter before him, to see what Colin's profession is*

	Could anything emotional or psychological . . . ?
Guru	*(a slight impatience)* Mr Harding: you do perform the sexual act?
Colin	Yes.
Guru	And you ejaculate?
Colin	Yes.
Guru	Well. Man's piddling little psyche might hinder performance, but not affect one whit the chemical quality of what he secretes. The trouble in your case most possibly lies with neither wife nor you, but in the combination of your two genetic chemistries. *(stands)* You are familiar with the routine for the post-coital test?
Colin	We have done several. *(stands)*
Guru	*(looks at letter)* Here also your diligence has been excessive: there is no need for the alarmclock, intercourse the night before is quite sufficient.

> *Receptionist re-enters, making Anne present again; Guru bringing Colin up above behind her:*

Semen is petrol, the engine is the womb: the one must merely be brought, effective, to the other. I recommend you now, during the fertile period of Mrs Harding's month, to adopt for intercourse what I call a posture of performing dogs—

> *Receptionist charmingly invites: Anne poses as Guru describes:*

Your wife on her knees, head down, her buttocks spread—

Anne	*(to us)* Dignity.

> *Receptionist bows Anne's head; Guru brings Colin behind her—*

Guru	You entering from behind. Which may, in your case, revive certain unorthodox memories. Nevertheless—

> *Motions Colin to kneel closer behind Anne, almost*

to mount her. Receptionist meanwhile brings a larger-than-life anatomy-class cross-sectioned phallus, a similar model of female genitalia:

You will see how, in this posture, the female tackle flops, affording the penis—

Receptionist inserts phallus: a clicking of parts—

—the most efficient angle of insemination. Compared with which, the conventional Anglo-American attitude—

Receptionist withdraws phallus, Guru rights corset: Receptionist inserts again, click click click—

—from the spermatozoön's point of view, is all uphill.

Colin and Anne remain postured: clinical objects.

Guru	It's all yours.
Colin	You'll send us the bill?
Receptionist	Of course.

Receptionist and Guru go. Colin starts in—Guru re-emerges:

Guru   Mr Harding, one other thing. We may of course be wrong in assuming your sperm count adequate—

Colin, interrupted—

I'm not altogether satisfied with the procedure at that clinic—

Receptionist follows, bringing to Colin a specimen-jar of contrasting, but equally impractical, design:

Would you, therefore, as early as you feel able, observing the necessary three days' continence beforehand, be good enough to furnish a sample at your home, returning it well sealed to me by post, first class? I can then do a count myself before I come to the PC test to see what, if anything, ill-befalls your semen in your wife.

Guru goes, Receptionist follows.
Colin stands away with vessel, addressing us:

Colin   Up again, down again : Jack found fecund, now his fecundity in question, now branded barren. *(Developing a tone of mocking self-laceration)* So, if Jack's lust does after all lack living spore, this seems to Jack wondrous like Nature does not select him for the Club of Man—the sort, I mean, Nature prefers not to continue his kind. I learned to live with *that* emotion a long time since. Yet: might not Nature's very discardment of Jack rank Jack a little higher than the genital beast in Man? *More* man than Reproductive Man? Paradox.

Think. Jack's seed, quâ sterile, is fit for transcendental sport alone; made, not for breeding, but delight alone; to be shot singing out, anarchic, athletic, milk in itself, free up vagina and glad up lad-arse, knob leaving cunt for joy alone, splitting sphincter and reaming rectum for joy alone, his bags drained dry through holes in walls by unseen men's mouths: the naked jissom, dis-Communion-ized, for play alone. *(Quieter)* Perhaps there is some sort of evolution here: man's sex emancipated from the shackle and the mire of Propagation; a sexuality dis-familied, detribalized, *fraternal*: in this sterility, the seed of that?

> *Colin goes up to bed, kneels behind Anne upon it; wearily they posture themselves.*

Anne   He functions to order every time. Only once, for the Guru's PC, he couldn't stay hard, it wouldn't penetrate—Surprised? You try it to order on two or three fixed nights in the cycle: knowing "Tonight or never; the love-blend must be there for the doctor tomorrow; or for hope of conception this month. Or for doctor anyway." In this posture. He probably has to pretend I'm some sailor from his misspent youth.

Colin   *(makes to mount her)* The acts don't resemble, lovey. Though it is possible to fantasize: which, frankly, at times has helped me. *(Suddenly sighs, falls away, lies wretched)*

Anne   Anyway, this one time, for the Guru's PC, he just couldn't stay hard enough to enter. Every effort of mine just made him floppier.

> *She slowly meanwhile rests back upon her hunkers, more and more relaxing him, generating simply by tenderness and voice a deeply erotic mood:*

But in the night, in his sleep, he was starting me. I woke up so turned on. After a while I went down on him—it was the first time I had ever been moved to do that. He'd come up very heavy and strong: the knob felt so burgeoning and gorgeous. So, half-asleep, we managed it after all. So we've never, in all these years—for doctor or calendar—never once failed to deliver. On occasions like the one I describe, he can be quite a satyr. Appearances deceive.

Colin   It's better at such times, love, the better you help me.

Anne   *(not breaking mood till very end)* I thought after that one, I thought if the quality of the act itself has anything to do with it and we haven't clicked this time, then there's no fucking justice in the thing. *(Bitterly lies away)*

> *Cancel Colin. Guru comes, brisk, quiet to Anne; gently, firmly postures her (turned on to left side, right leg crooked up). Anne, to us:*

This man is a *specialist*. He examines in the Sims position. Not like your National Health.

> *Lies so for examination. Guru makes minimal sufficient gestures of examination: touch, palp, pressure, etc.*

Guru　　Your husband's sperms are now of normal vitality, Mrs Harding. Yet by the time they percolate here—*(pats her lower belly)*—a great proportion of them are dead. You would seem to be killing your husband's semen, Mrs Harding: why is that?

> *There has been no cruelty in his tone, merely a philosophical mildly rebuking gentleness. Anne can say nothing.*

The medical profession has no answer in such a case. It may be, that some form of chemical rejection is taking place—

Anne　　*(clutching at joyous straw)* Something to do with antigens?

Guru　　*(looks at her stilly, says nothing. Then)* This is a terra incognita of medical science. There is a broader possibility. In intercourse the vagina produces a self-protective acid. Sperms do not like this acid. The acid, therefore, not only helps prevent infection, it also acts as a goad to the sperms to hasten them on their way. Perhaps your vagina is producing too much acid, or too strong. Relax . . . *(comes away, to sit behind desk. Quiet, to self:)* So many good spermatozoa dead.

Anne　　*(relaxes up, semi-sitting)* Massacre of the Innocents.

Guru　　Unjust, yes. Your doing, but not your fault.

Anne　　If I shove my fanny full of bicarb before we sex, would that do any good? *(comes to desk)*

Guru　　*(does not like being anticipated)* I was coming to the alkaline douche. *(Brings from a drawer in desk a package)* This, is a little something of my own invention. Bicarbonate of soda is, yes, safe, and domestically available. But do remember you thereby expose your vagina to infection. So be moderate. *(Gives package)*

Anne　　*(sitting)* Maybe we should just accept our infertility as our part played in easing an overpopulated world.

Guru　　And be content to leave the breeding to village yobs, clapped-out royalty and Papish slums? While the psychopaths that misgovern our globe make waste and slag of its sufficiency?

Anne　　I don't like to think of people in terms of absolute worth.

Guru　　Then start to think so. You know your Malthus as well as I do: the one inheritance Man is short in is Reason. Even if you and your husband look like the back ends of buses, you've more than an average share of Reason to bequeath. That is your duty to the world. If Man is to survive, he must evolve up out of his mythic mire; and soon. So tell your husband to keep up the cold water treatment and the diet; and you combine the posture and the alkali. We'll get you a bun in the oven for Hogmanay. *(briskly goes)*

Colin   *(discovered on bed)* Another seven old guineas, that sets us back.

> *Anne undoes package: a comically flopping douche device:*

Anne   And this, another two. *(Squeezes nozzle, makes gurgling sounds with mouth)*

> *Colin comes to her. They lark with douche; suddenly, as though afraid of losing their sexuality for ever, are in desperate, almost childish play.*

I wish we could get back to sex for kicks.

Colin   *(Guru voice)* "You are not one of those fortunates, Mrs Harding, that can conceive with 'kicks': accept that. You might yet need recourse to my Inseminator, a Heath Robinson device I've invented for ferrying live sperms through no-go areas."

> *Mood suddenly broken: Anne remembers what the douche is for. Colin: new note of hardness ill-suppressed:*

Give fanny her gargle, then.

> *Anne goes off with douche.*

While I lie, lashing up salacious thoughts of utmost crudity to sustain my erection, my heart knocks like a stone with the false effort . . . Till you come from the bathroom, cold as ice—

> *Anne returns, adopts posture on bed—*

Anne   To squat before my lord, my arse on high like Table Mountain. *(To us)* All grey in the dark. *(i.e. all cats' arses are grey, etc.)*

Colin   *(raises self on knees behind her)* And I must start upon her straightaway . . . *(Reaches hands beneath her oxters)* And get my pint pulled up you straightaway—

Anne   Being not sure how long or short the antacid effect of the bicarb will last—

Colin   To say nothing of the fact this bloody posture is giving me piles—

> *Cut light off. In darkness, loud on speakers: sounds of a fruit machine being played, rhythmic, dry, mechanical, luckless. Up light.*

Anne   Why can't we make like the amoeba?

Colin   Split in two?

Anne   Or freeze in a cyst, then explode in little hundreds.

Colin	Defeat the object, wouldn't it?
Anne	What is the object?

They remain coupled, motionless, faces towards us.

Colin	To think we were a year on the pill before we married.
Anne	*(to us)* Repeat on the thirteenth and fifteenth nights of the cycle. Two cycles. Five.
Colin	*(slowly withdrawing)* Remembering always to come away carefully, not spilling any. *(Lies away from her, speaking over pillow to us:)* Sacrament my arse. Four stages of a childless marriage. "Children?" *(Mild)* "Not yet." "Children?" *(Slightly rebuking)* "Give us time." "Children?" *(Gentle, sad)* "No." "Children?" *(Defiant, i.e. Should there be?)* "No."
Anne	*(relaxes up into Little Mermaid pose, drawing blanket round herself, facing off)* "Try changing the wallpaper," they say. Aunts, mother-in-law, sisters. "It's nothing to do with the *function*," I tell them; "that part of it's all right."

Now appears behind her a Young Married, Valerie, pushing a pram and obscenely pregnant, a mixture of the affected-vulgar and intellectual pretension:

Valerie	Try buying some different-coloured nighties, dear.
Anne	I've told you, Valerie: that part's in order!
Valerie	Get him away, a romantic holiday, a second honeymoon—or would it be the third or fourth, dear, including those you had with him before you were married?
Anne	It's nothing—
Valerie	George had his troubles, too. A warm climate's the thing—

Colin, as being discussed behind his back, slinks unhappy off.

Anne	It's chemistry, Valerie. Not the sex, the chemistry.
Valerie	Perhaps he should take up football. On second thoughts perhaps not, knowing his past. *(Continues off)*
Anne	*(almost tearful)* It's nothing to do with that! It's chemistry! *(Settles in blanket again)* Women. Young Marrieds. Shriek to each other across their prams. Joggle their dummy-stuffed spoils of the sex war up and down. Trundle along their suburban bellies bloated with the booty of the bed. "How far are you on, then, Doreen? Five months? Oh, I'm six." Cows. The only function they're up to, so they crack it high: cows, cows. They look at me. "*You* haven't pillaged your breadwinner's basket in the dark when he thinks he's polishing the top sheet with his arse; *you* haven't ignited a brat; *you*'re no woman, *you*'re inadequate." I get to hate my parasitic sex.

Now comes down past them to desk a Gynaecological Surgeon: smooth, groomed, impeccably dressed in conservative fashion. He has a medical file, quite full by now. Colin, Anne assemble themselves.

Surgeon   But in all these years of consultation, no one has thought to confirm if you are in fact ovulating, Mrs Harding. *(To us)* Gynaecological surgeon, their last resort. *(Sits behind desk)*

Colin, Anne come down, sit: she opposite Surgeon, Colin at desk-end between them.

No point in pumping your poor husband dry, if there is no egg for him to fertilize. *(takes slim packet from drawer)* So, with your next cycle, you must begin a regular taking of your morning temperature on waking, entering it each day with a cross on this chart. *(Brings out from drawer a quarto buff envelope, from which he takes blank temperature-charts—for stage purposes, somewhat larger than they would really be)*.

Colin, Anne furtively glance at each other, reduced.

If, round about your tenth day or so, the graph you are making suddenly dips, say five or six points of a degree, and the next day rises again by as much and a little more, you can normally assume ovulation has occurred. Whereupon I recommend you two to initiate an orgy. After six months, if you have indeed not conceived before then, make an appointment to bring me the charts, so that I can see what ovulation-pattern, if any, is suggested by them. It is helpful also if you ring the graph-points on dates when intercourse has taken place. *(Looks at top letter in file)* Bicarbonate of soda. Yes. Used in moderation, possibly quite helpful; though useless of course without ovulation, I think you understand that. Antacid effectiveness in the vagina, lasts quite some hours. You could douche yourself at leisure during the evening; earlier, even. *(Glances down at letter again, to take up the next of the points that they have queried there:)* Posture. Circus dogs, you call it. *(Shakes head)* Unless you enjoy it that way. It makes mechanical sense, but has not, in my experience, significantly increased the chances of conception in a case like yours. One thing your letter does not make clear: your sperm counts, were they of motility only? Not of volume?

Colin   Not of volume. That I know of.

Surgeon   I don't mean the quantity of the load, I mean its density in sperms. Your sperms can be the most motile under heaven, but if they are few, say a mere fifty million per millilitre, then all the cold water in the world will not make you fertile.

Colin   I know the drill.

Surgeon *(bringing up from drawer a long, printed envelope that slightly bulges)* Good. The more sperms you put into circulation at any one time, the better your chances, I think you see that. The contents are self-explanatory: two forms, a sealable container. By post to the Path Lab, or drop it by: for this purpose a time-lag will not matter; even if all the sperms die in the post, it is merely a question of our counting the corpses.

Colin takes envelope, Anne charts.

If that, and these, are in order, I see no reason why the two of you should not be expectant by midsummer.

Colin You will send the bill.

Surgeon Yes. And the charts and the thermometer together will come to an extra eighty pence. *(Stands, quiet, to go)* Don't be despondent.

Goes. Lightchange. Anne to bedfoot, with charts, pencil, thermometer. Colin remains in halflight, seated at desk-end.

Anne Sixteenth of February, sixth day of cycle: ninety-seven point nine, sexed. *(With thermometer, seems to trace her entries on chart)* Seventeenth of February, ninety-seven point seven. Eighteenth of February, blank: faulty thermometer. Ninth day of cycle, new thermometer, temperature ninety-eight. Ninety-seven point nine, sexed. Point six. Point six. Blank—dropped thermometer. Ninety-eight ... Sixteenth day of cycle, up: ninety-nine point three. Point two, sexed; sore throat and cold; point four ... Four, three, three ... Twenty-eighth day of cycle, point eight again. Period.

Colin bleakly looks across at Anne's bowed head, hard in spite of himself. She scans charts as though for sign of life; finds none. To us:

They assure us it's neither's *fault*. Yet now it seems because of his deficiency, now because of mine. That gets at you. The combination of our chemistries, they say. Yet now it seems his fault, now it seems mine.

Sits with charts, demoralized. Colin, at desk-end, mimes speech into phone:

Colin I want only to find out if you have the *result* yet. . . . But it has been rather a long time— . . . It was not a motility test, madam, it was a density test— . . . Hell, the analysis must surely have been done by now, the figures must be some-where. . . . I am not trying, madam, to tell Pathology their job; I merely wish you would credit other professions than yours with some scintilla of intelligence. . . . All I want to know— *(pause)* I appreciate you cannot tell me over the public line. Even if we could be sure the line was not tapped I accept entirely your reason for that: but I am not asking for the result, I am merely trying to establish whether there yet is one, and when my doctor can expect to receive it. *(Pause)* I *am* aware your wheels rotate at an inflexible speed—God, this is England all over: *(Bitter mimicry)* "We must preserve an empty mind"—Can you merely estimate roughly how long, from donation of sample, a man must wait for the alimentary process of your hospital to excrete a result?—For the Lord's sake, woman, it *is my sperm* . . .

> *Re-enter, simply, quiet to desk, Surgeon with a letter:*

Surgeon Excellent. Perfectly satisfactory. Average, not more; but normally fertile. What more could you reasonably demand?

> *Colin, Anne meanwhile sit before him. Surgeon turns to Anne and her envelope:*

Now, here what have we? What are these?

> *Anne shoves charts before him. Surgeon cannot join them up; he seems to find them scruffy. Suddenly Anne is as vulnerable as a pathetic slum child before an irascible teacher.*

How do these connect?

> *Anne tries to organize them; they become a muddle.*

February . . . Where is March?

> *Anne, Surgeon search in vain. Colin, Anne clumsily change places.*

This blot: what happened here?

Anne Thermometer broke.

Surgeon April . . . Where is March?

> *Colin watches this with tense amazement and annoyance. Surgeon points:*

What are these diamonds?

Anne *(peers)* Pencil broke. It broke when I was doing a circle. For when we'd sexed. So I turned the circle into a diamond. Because of the scratch. So I turned them all into diamonds.

> *Surgeon holds up chart: it is studded with diamond-marks clustered in fours and fives midcycle, blank elsewhere. Then:*

Surgeon Where is March?

> *It is found. Surgeon arranges charts:*

Now we have a chronology. *(Waves to Anne to sit near him where she can follow)* Yes . . . *(ponders)* A slightly erratic ovulation-pattern; but it is there. Look, March; then July; this month . . . —You're still on the water?

Colin   *(suddenly stammering)* Y—es. Two minutes every—

Surgeon   *(to her)* And the antacid douche?

Colin   Just as you t— As you t—old us, yes—

> *Irrational long pause.*

Surgeon   Well. *(Pause)* Well then, why aren't we conceiving? All that, in conjunction with these . . . *(i.e. charts)*

Colin   *(sudden nervous fatuity)* It's all rather like planning a moon-shot.

Surgeon   *(ignores him)* With all this, the odds now are, you should hit the jackpot before the end of the year. I frankly see nothing else I nor anyone can do, except leave it to Nature's blind will, with your rational assistance. *(Collects charts, clips them in file)* You have approached the problem with realism and courage: I am sure your pertinacity will be rewarded.

> *Lightdim, Surgeon quietly going.*

Colin   *(turning "through" us)* Aye. In time to pick up our Pensions on the way.

> *Darkness. Soon, shapes of Colin asleep on bed, Anne, semi-cumbent, beside him. Anne has thermometer in mouth, then reads it. Soon she begins to cluck like a hen. Colin wakes, stirs:*

What's up wi' you?

Anne   I've laid an egg. I've laid an egg!

Colin   Hang out the flags.

Anne   *(rising over him)* An innocent ovum: has descended the Fallopian. Come and get it.

Colin   I see. I'm in for a week of phallic martyrdom then, am I?

> *Darkness. On speakers, fruitmachine sounds. Suddenly a triumphant cataclasm of money. Cut. Voices of Doctor and Jennifer call across dark stage to each other:*

Doctor   Jennifer?

Jennifer   Doctor?

Doctor   Mrs Harding's urine sample: did you test it?

Jennifer   Yes.

Doctor   What shall I tell her?

Jennifer   Tell her Positive.

> *Organ, orchestra, choir titanically burst out: first*

half-dozen bars Mahler VIII "Veni, veni Creator Spiritus". Up pencilspot on desk now draped altar-like with white cloth, central on it a tall specimen-jar, chalice-like, filled with straw-coloured liquid. Tighten spot on jar till it glows like Holy Grail. Brutally, in mid-paean, cut music, light. Silence, darkness.

Follow as soon as practically possible with:

II

Bare piano-octave rapidly reiterated, clattering empty, grim: Schubert's Der ErlKönig. *(In the darkness strike the jar, cloth and desk.) Fade before singer heard; up stonechat-finch-song—discreetly softcentred sound, intentionally "lyrical". Up warm sunlight. Anne lies in smock on naked ground (NB no blanket), Colin in trousers, open shirt, up of her, lazily stroking her belly. The tenderness is between the three of them: man, woman, unborn child. He tries to remember words of a poem (in fact Traherne's "Salutation"), can manage only a halting garble:*

Colin   *(to self)* What shall this be? That out of nothing comes . . . Who, dust a thousand years . . . did in a chaos lie . . . *(Puts ear to her belly. His caress and wonder broaden, including Anne herself. After a moment, softly whistles a strain of "Brigg Fair".* Suddenly, to us:)* So bloody English, this. All we need's a bit of Delius offstage.

Cuckoo afar. If it makes audience feel intellectually superior to dramatist, so much the better.

Anne   *(unstirring)* There's a man in the South somewhere, has a cuckoo in a cage. He takes it out into his garden every spring, so that people can hear it and write to *The Times*.

Colin's stroking begins to show sexual intent—

                Not here, love—

Colin   Why?

Anne   People—

Colin   Who? Who's to see? No one comes up *this* hill any more—

Anne   *(mock Northern)* Officer wi' telescope.

Colin   Let him. *(Careful of Anne's precious burden, becomes more sexually purposeful—)*

Anne   *(shifts in sudden discomfort)* Trouble with being Lawrentian. Ants and—spines . . . Sorry, love, I'll have to pee first. This weight.

Colin   A heavy bladder is a stimulus to me.

Anne   Difference between us. *(Moving from him—)*

Colin   *(draws her firmly down)* I'm damn glad we're *not* the amoeba.

They deepkiss. After a long moment Anne goes up, off, waddling slightly. Colin lies languorous; with

* See Appendix.

discreet private gesture, fingers luxuriously stretched and hooking, suggests the deep still glory of his resurrected shaft, reburgeoned testicles. Searches memory for poem again:

Who shall . . . who shall he or she be . . . ? That out of nothing comes . . . A nothing : that all a sudden—is . . . Where there was empty darkness, a sudden eye, seeing . . . Sudden in emptiness, new-minted limbs. Out of the dark silence, a forming tongue . . . Child—*(Ulsterish)* Jamie . . . or *(Ulsterish)* Annie . . .

Silence. Anne emerging, afraid to move.
Something wrong. Colin turns sharply to her—

Anne   *(quiet, hard)* No sex. Get me home. I'm passing these. *(She thrusts into his, our sight, a white tissue in her cupped hands. In it, black clots of blood)*

A moment. Shock goes off in Colin like a deep mine —no other reaction shown. Cut light. (Or, in slow lightchange, Colin brings heavily home "indoors" again, e.g. the haversack they had taken out with them; there, in gloomy light, begins to make bed—its foot toward us now—for:) Anne coming, careful how she moves, in a white nightdress now. Eases herself carefully on to, into bed. Colin off, Doctor (of opening scenes) coming: black case, short driving-coat. (Aside, an upright chair, on which jacket, tie, etc.)

Doctor   *(quiet)* How far are you on now, Mrs Harding ?
Anne   Three months.
Doctor   Well ; this is what we call a Pregnancy at Risk.
Anne   What must we do ?
Doctor   Stay in bed until forty-eight hours after the bleeding stops.
Anne   It will stop ?
Doctor   It'll have to stop some time. You haven't an inexhaustible supply. *(Quietly goes off)*

Lightchange, Colin coming slowly down with a wicker waste-basket full with dark-stained, bloody tissues:

Colin   *(to us)* And such blood. The clots of it, claret-colour, solid-soft. The child is lost. I don't mean I foresee that—we'll do everything mortal possible to prevent that. I mean, it is now that in the heart the loss takes place. *(He is going to say something more. Decides not to. Goes up slowly toward bed with basket)*

Lightchange, Doctor comes quietly, in hat, with

> *case. Anne lies under bedclothes, head on high*
> *pillow, facing us. Doctor rests bag on bed:*

Doctor   So what happened this time, Mrs Harding?

Anne   I lay as you said. The blood stopped. It dried. It came up brown and fibry. I saved you—

> *She makes as to bring out a tissue with it from under*
> *pillow—Doctor gestures no need—*

Thank God we got the spuds in before this happened.

Doctor   Spuds in already?

Anne   He uses the Ulster calendar. In Patrick's day, out Billy's day. Well, then I got up. I helped put in the tomato plants—well, *that*'s not strenuous.

Colin   *(returning, hovers with basket) I* did the digging. I thought this year to water the soil very heavily at the start. Drive the roots down . . . *(Realizes he is chattering. Puts basket by bed, goes off)*

Anne   In the night I felt wet. Blood again: red, bright; fresh. Bed-rest. Dry again; forty-eight clear hours, then up again. *No* exertion this time. We're going out. I clean myself up. Blood again. Bed again. Dry again, up again, blood again; bed again. Doctor, that drug—there's a drug—

Doctor   Our pharmacy shelves are full of that, we never prescribe it now. It seals you up. If you *insist* . . . But if there's a good reason for a foetus to miscarry then miscarry we must let it. I know you have very much wanted this child, but you at least know now how you can conceive.

Anne   I'm not that young.

Doctor   Nonsense.

Anne   If it takes that long again I'll be over thirty. What you call it— an "elderly primate"?* Superannuated ape.

Doctor   You won't find a good apple dropped from a tree. If that sounds like corny rural wisdom, it is nevertheless so. Things happen in their time.

Anne   Doctor, what chance?

Doctor   Fifty-fifty.

Anne   As bad as that?

Doctor   Try to keep calm. Stay in bed now. *(closes bag, goes)*

> *Colin, paler-faced, wheels in a Variett-style table—*
> *height adjustable: on it, cereals in dish, a boiled egg,*
> *bread, coffee-pot, marmalade. A new day.*

Colin   *(slightly hard)* How's the blood?

Anne   *(takes clean tissue from under pillow; explores with it*

---

* See Appendix.

beneath blanket; withdraws it) Started again. *(Shows him reddened tissue, almost flinching)*

Colin   *(face hard, still. Wheels table so that it lies across her like a tray)* I'm not sure about the egg.

Anne   What do you mean, "not sure about the egg"?—

Colin   Well, it's the second one. The first floated. Even this one tried to turn its beam end up.

Anne   *(sees it is missing)* Salt.

Colin   Sorry. *(Goes)*

Anne   *(shouts after)* I don't like the eggs from Clay Hall Farm, they taste of fish. God knows what they feed their poultry on. *(Sprays sugar on cereal)*

       Colin comes with salt—

Darling, I'm sorry, you've forgotten the spoon.

Colin   Sorry. *(Goes)*

Anne   *(shouts)* Why don't you get the eggs from Clink Farm? *(Crunches teeth into cereal)*

Colin   *(returns with teaspoon)* Because Clink is out of my way. *(Snatches tie from chair, half-threads it on—)*

Anne   Oh, not that spoon, dear, for eggs; they stain. The Apostle spoons.

Colin   Sorry, I didn't think. *(Goes)*

Anne   *(shouts)* Well, how many times have you eaten an egg and not noticed what spoon you're using?

Colin   *(returns)* Judas, that do you? I'll go and have my own now—

       Tray tilts over, spilling; Anne, screaming, saves coffee-pot, egg, holds these transfixed—

That's all I need.

Anne   Who didn't tighten the sodding screw?

       Colin rights tray, tightens screw; restores what order he can. Bread-and-butter loathsomely dirtied on floor.

You're treading the cornflakes in—

Colin   Well, either you— *(i.e. want me to tighten the table—)*

Anne   Well don't. Oh, hell, there's milk on the blankets—*

Colin   Well I'm sorry—Use a tissue—A tissue—! *(etc.)*

Anne   It'll come through to the sheets,* love. I can't lie in wet sheets: sponge it off, quickly—A sponge, love; quickly—! *(etc.)*

       Colin exits, Anne dabs with tissues. Colin returns with sponge. They dab.

       * See Appendix.

Colin	You'll need more milk now. *(Goes)*
Anne	I'll eat the cornflakes dry, I'll drink the coffee black !
Colin	*(off)* Don't be silly.

> *Anne begins breakfast. From Colin, off, an unnecessarily loud cry of despair.*

	Oh no ! No !
Anne	*(shouts)* What is it ?
Colin	*(off, furious)* Out. Out. Out ! *Out!* (Pause)
Anne	What's happened ?
Colin	*(comes with milk bottle)* Excuse jug. Two pieces of news. First the good. The cat, has puked. *(Goes off)*
Anne	Feed her properly, she won't.
Colin	*(off)* She's perfectly fittingly fed.
Anne	You give her too much hardtack.
Colin	*(off)* We're out of tins
Anne	Get some on the way home, then. Christ. Hardtack's bad for them all the time. Hallucinogenic.
Colin	*(enters with dustpan, brush)* What ?
Anne	It blows their feline minds. Doctor was saying : three weeks on that hardtack and their cat was found cowering in front of a mouse.
Colin	*(brushes up floor round bed)* Now for the bad news. What I found in the vomit. A goldfinch head.*
Anne	Oh no.
Colin	She's eaten one of the goldfinches from the tree. The other is fluttering around demented.
Anne	Oh no.
Colin	Stupid bitch of a cat. It'd be tolerable if she'd at least done it the honour of digesting it. Most beautiful songbird in Europe, what a waste. They chose our garden for their home. At their nesting they worked so hard. Collaborated so well. For their eggs and— *(Silence)*
Anne	Better go and clean it up. *(Takes clean tissue, explores)*
Colin	I've not the time now. *(Tie half-tied, snatches jacket—)*
Anne	It'll stink the place out, flies'll come in, it'll stain— *(Brings out tissue; very red)*
Colin	I'm supposed to be playing for Assembly this morning. *(Sees tissue, offers waste-basket)* Your egg'll be cold.
Anne	*(wipes hand on blanket-corner)* I don't want it.
Colin	Eat it. You're getting no lunch, you know that. *(Goes out with dustpan, brush)*

* See Appendix.

Anne   *(taps egg)* Egg smells funny. *(Beheads egg with knife.*
                Suddenly a most convulsive recoil—she hurls herself from
                bed, reels down—with a shock we see her nightdress stained
                where she bleeds. Crouches shuddering, utterly upturned)

                        Colin re-enters; sees her gone; looks into egg. Utters
                        almost inaudible choke of abomination; covers egg
                        with first thing to hand; stands, bottling nausea,
                        shock.

Anne   *(to self)* What am I trying to save? Some monster to be born,
                they'll take one look at—

                        Colin stumbles away out with egg. Lightchange:
                        Anne feels belly, wondering what horror might be
                        forming there:

                Or a Mozart, Darwin? My will is blind. But is it itself willed,
                by some other Will, that *sees*? That wills into being—Man's
                share of monstrosity or his share of light? Is it either of these?
                Or is the world's will wild? Without mercy, senseless? At
                the heart of things, what if there *is* no purpose, no logic, no
                love at all?

                        Lightchange, to lower area: Anne donning plain
                        dressing-gown, Colin comes bringing a garden-
                        lounger, unfolds this, erects it downstage; dressed as
                        returned from school.

Colin   *(no sarcasm)* Have you thought how lucky we are? Unlike
                the Mrs Seenys of this world: blessed by her bishop, no
                doubt, in whelping a degenerating line of brats she's neither
                intelligence, courage nor moral conscience to contracevie.
                And on our rates. *(Brings bedclothes down)* Think how
                lucky. We know exactly *how* to click, and that's so damn
                roundabout a method, the thing itself really is "Love without
                Fear". Think of the rabbit. She ovulates every time she's
                entered. Homo sapiens is at least some way advanced on
                that. Perhaps you and I and others in our predicament are one
                stage even more evolved.

Anne   *(eases self carefully on to lounger)* Right now I'd rather be
                an ammonite.

Colin   *(tucks her in)* Extinction hurts, too. We're wrong to patronize
                the dinosaur, by the way. One of the kids was saying. The
                dinosaur lasted five hundred times longer than Man is
                likely to. It seems Man's last end, though, will be the moral
                same. *(Tidies bedclothes away)*

Anne   Out of step with his environment.

Colin   Worse than that. It seems there were tiny termites, millions
                of them, eating their way up the Dinosaur's legs. His nerve-
                system was so slow, out of touch with his condition, the

pain didn't reach the brain till all his nethers were eaten away.

Anne reaches out another bloodied tissue, Colin automatically brings down waste-basket:

So what are *our* termites? What danger-signal is the *human* brain not getting? *(Goes)*

Valerie (young married from Act I) breezes down in:

Valerie   Coo-ee, folks!
Anne   *(mixed feelings)* Valerie?
Valerie   The door was open. *(She is not pregnant now)* Anne, my love, you look so pale!

Her cruelty throughout this scene is pure animal: she deceives her better self she is trying to make Anne feel a welcome new member to the suffering-wife-and-mother club; she would be ninety per cent horrified if someone were to tell her she was doing the cruel opposite.

I do hope Colin's cooking's not too awful.
Anne   Oh, his hand's well in now. It *has* been weeks. Anyway, he didn't come straight from his mother's arms to mine.
Valerie   *(brings chair, sits)* You must be ravenous, let me get you something.
Anne   It's the life of Riley. Honest. Oh, a very *Protestant* Riley . . . A curry or a carbonnade does two or three nights, on Fridays fish-and-chips from the van—
Valerie   Nothing very Protestant about fish on Fridays—My poor thing, you're looking so pale! You mustn't let him frazzle you. I know men. He'll try to make you feel guilty because he has to knuckle to for once like a domestic martyr; he'll look at you accusingly because you're out of action bleeding your guts out.
Anne   They're his guts as well in a way I'm bleeding out.
Valerie   Don't let him. You need calm, peace of mind. I'll make some coffee. *(Goes off)*
Anne   He was like that a bit at first. But he had it all to do: house, cooking, nursing, garden—examination term. He's very organized now though: real Time-and-Motion. "Stop and think." Before he does anything, "Stop and think". I've never seen him so still.

Crash of broken jug off—

Valerie   *(off, tearful voice)* Oh Anne, I'm so sorry. I'll pay you for it—no, I insist. Even if I have to scrub floors. *(Appears with frag-*

ment of blue-and-white Cornish pottery) I do hope it wasn't
sentimental. It says "Tintangle". Was that were you had one of
your honeymoons, dear?

Anne   That. Was already in his collection when I joined it. I think
         Tintagel was where he began drafting that big play of his;
         the one no one ever did.

Valerie Ah. His writing days. Old times. *(with fragment, out to
         kitchen)*

Anne   Heard about that man arrested in Brum the other day?
         Blowing bubbles in the street? He got fined. For "obstruc-
         tion". I want this previous little bastard, if he lives, to be a
         blower of bubbles, Christ I do. *(Quiet, more and more to
         self)* Oh, I don't know. You bring a kid up anarchist, he ends
         up joining the Police. How do you bring up a spirit to be free?
         Shove his tongue up the anus of Authority and trust to his
         instinct for revolt? Manipulation, that. Hell's teeth, why hang
         my hang-ups round the necks of the unborn? *(addressing
         belly)* Bloodbeast. Take over the graveyard in your own good
         time and your own right. If you see our values have failed us,
         cack on our graves.

              Valerie returns with coffee in cups on tray.

Valerie Look pleased to see me.
Anne   *(meaning no slight)* I'm pleased to see anybody, stuck like
         this.
Valerie Thank *you*!

              *They drink. Pause. Valerie: a new tone—a we-
              women-can't-win confidence is coming:*

         Speaking of bastards. *(pause)* You're not the only one with
         troubles. *I'm* over*due*. I shouldn't be saying this to you in
         your condition, but what I've been going through—! I don't
         want it, Anne; I can't have it; well I can't, can I? How can
         I? It isn't George's, it's Fred's. Oh, I *know* . . . What's so
         awful, we've only slept together once this cycle—

Anne   You have it easy, all you have to do is sleep together—!
Valerie But isn't it rotten, such rotten luck, Anne? Oh, Anne love,
         it's so *horrible* . . . *(in tears)* Here are you two, suffering all
         this time to get one even started, and you're not able to keep
         it in; here's Yours Truly racking her tiny brain how to get
         hers out on the scrapheap in time. It's a pig of a world, so
         unjust, I can't tell you how sorry for you both I am: I wake
         up thinking how pale you both are, your pale faces, and
         you were so healthy before you married and so *happy* . . . God,
         in the old days, Colin—*(tears forgotten)*—on that Lambretta—
         looking so brown—

Colin comes, utterly unselfconsciously tying on a woman's apron:

Colin   *(pointing)* Ah, *here*'s the tray—

Valerie   Colin! *(Sees apron; incredulous shriek:)* Colin! I never thought to see the day!

Colin   What? Oh this. *(Camps slightly, to trap her—)*

            Valerie utters a camp giggle, Anne wryly watches—

            Yes, you *would* think it funny. I just happen to be weird: I don't see how it is manlier somehow, to let one's clothes get wet. *(takes tray, leaving cups)*

Valerie   *(shouts after)* I didn't say anything about your not being virile, Colin! Lord, how should I know? *(Turns to Anne, resumes we-women-can't-win tune:)* God, the trouble I had, carrying Jason. He simply re*fused* to be born. George was driving me over level-crossings, foreways and backways; the little bugger simply *refused* to be born. Christ, when he did come, such a relief, my dear: to be able to see your toes again. *(Something—a sound from the kitchen, perhaps; or a perceptible withdrawal suddenly in Anne—makes Valerie feel redundant:)* Ah well. When you're up and about again, my dear, you must come and have tea with me and the children, and we'll have a jolly old cow. *(stands, whispers)* Don't let him *frazzle* you, dear. *(Calls)* By-ee! *(Goes)*

            Colin emerges, jabs thumb in her departed direction:

Colin   When my mother was in the Royal Victoria having that breast off, there was an old biddy from Ballymacarrett sat up on high pillows opposite her all the day, dangling *(gestures)* her full pair over the bedclothes. For cruelty, of all the sexes, women are the worst. *(Kisses Anne, takes cups, goes)*

            Anne, questioningly, feels her belly; is troubled. Colin comes, sits on chair, aproned still.

Colin   *(quiet)* I never know what I'll find instead of you when I get home. And at night: I sleep deeper than hell, yet the slightest shift of you, I'm full sharp awake—*(pause)*

Anne   It wakes me, too, the blood.

Colin   My frazzle didn't make you any better. My frazzle at the beginning is part of the fault of it.

Anne   *(to disabuse him)* I lost a little at the *second* month.

            Each suddenly conscious of irremediable personal separateness.

Colin   My anxiety made you worse. That's why I slowed up. Anyway, we can have wrong things invested in a child.

Anne   I know.

Colin   If he or she is born, then he or she is born. If it is a matter of
         your will only, he shall be born. It's easy for me. I've every-
         thing to do. You've nothing but to lie, lie, willing. *(Would pat
         her belly—)*

Anne   *(gently stays his hand. Pause)* I think it's died.

                    Long silence.

         (helpless) There isn't the little flutter any more.

Colin   *(at last)* Maybe it's just lying quiet a while. They do that,
         don't they? *(Pause)* Or playing possum. Perhaps he's
         realized, it's life or death: so he just daren't rock the boat—
         too—vigorously . . . *(Pause. Brisk)* What simple task for you
         can I find, won't overtax your inferior domestic-female mind?
         *(Goes. Reappears with bowl of washed spuds, saucepan,
         spudbasher, newspaper for peelings)* For thick wife: "Put
         ze rett triankles in ze rett boxes, and ze green ones in ze
         green boxes."

                    *Anne seizes spudbasher in fist, pulls a stone-age
                    idiot gesture. Colin sits on chair Valerie has left.
                    They begin peeling.*

         That Eysenck book, by the way. The know-your-own-IQ
         one. I found a mistake. Well, not a mistake so much: an
         omission. Very revealing. He has a question: "Fill in ze
         missink letters. H, E, blank, I, T, A, blank, E."

Anne   *(thinks. Does her idiot act)* Artichoke.

                    They peel on a few moments.

Colin   No, think. *(writes with finger on paper)* H E blank I T A
         blank E.

Anne   *(studies paper as though letters were present there. At last)*
         I can do the picture ones, I can't do the word ones. I'm
         illiterate, I can't spell English, I didn't do any Latin at school.

Colin   *(pause. Exaggerated Ulster tone)* H. E. Blank. I. T. A. Blank.
         E.

Anne   *(immediate)* Heritage.

Colin   Heritage. So I thought. But not Our Father Eysenck. For him,
         the word is Hesitate. Let us anatomize the Eysenckian uni-
         verse. The planet Heritage does not so much as flicker in it.
         For Eysenckian man Inheritance does not exist—except as a
         congenital tic. In behaviourist Utopia we do not belong, we
         conform; we do not inherit, we obey. In Eysenckania, we
         each look vertically up, and up alone, parched lips straining
         for one normalizing eucharistic drop from the chalice of
         Paternalist Authority. Who does not crave so, electric treatment
         shall put right. Heritage my arse. He-si-tate. To stutter to

stammer to stumble to *be unsure, that,* in the Eysenck cosmos, is our determined rôle.

Anne Perhaps he just forgot.

Colin The man who'd speak from Sinai, has no business"forgetting".

Anne *(gently)* Did you switch 'oven on?

> *Colin has forgotten; goes. Anne quietly moves paper, peelings a little down; rests hand on belly. Uneasy. From under pillow takes out a clean tissue. Makes a cautious assay beneath blanket. Brings tissue out: no visible stain, yet something on it she does not like. She looks carefully, fearfully sniffs. Folds tissue carefully, stows into dressing-gown pocket (to keep for the Doctor). Settles to continue peeling, uneasy. After a moment tries to steepen headrest behind her head but, without knowing, jerks it too far forward before resting it carefully back at what she thinks is a new angle. Does not lean back immediately but brings paper, peelings, potatoes, etc., back into reach. Leans back, headrest falls flat, she with it. After a moment she sees she will have to ease self off lounger to adjust headrest. Clumsily, not daring to bend her body, she manoeuvres stiff self sideways off lounger—her foot fouls spudbowl; spuds, water spill; she collapses on to knees amid wet and dirt, heavy, crumpled, breathless. Colin comes quietly, sees.*

Colin *(annoyed she didn't call for help)* You hopeless woman. *(Starts to clear mess)*

Anne I'm all wet.

Colin You've coggled the bowl, I'm not surprised you're wet.

Anne *(without turning to him, hand to belly)* No, *here* I'm wet.

> *Pause.*

My waters have broken.

> *Turns her face up to him. A still moment. Ambulance Driver, gentle, heavy-sized, comes unfolding a stretcher. Colin goes to collect what Anne will need in hospital: no flap with him, all is smooth now. Driver lays stretcher out on floor between bed and lounger.*

Driver *(deeper rural accent, perhaps Birmingham-tarnished, than Doctor had)* Now don't you worry, dear. We'll get you there quick as we can. By the smooth road. We know all the bumps in the County, don't you worry. *(gently helps Anne on to stretcher)* This lady now sees, for the first time she fully

sees: she'm in danger of death. Some'at about our sympathy,
in how familiar we are with her condition, in how serious and
careful it makes us of her, strikes the scale from her eyes.
(Brings a red blanket to spread over Anne) From her bed,
from her room, from her little house now we bring her, gentle,
gentle on the stretcher . . . Easy then, Albert. Easy . . . *(He
draws stretcher backwards, Anne's head first, toward rostrum)* Out to the ambulance . . . Ambulance: common enough
thing, you say. But to her, to this woman, this ambulance is
the valley of the shadow, that sad little shadow through
which one in five of British mothers pass.

> *Climbs backward up on to rostrum as though up
> step into ambulance itself: raises stretcher-head, to
> display Anne to us like a straw guy. undignified,
> helpless:*

Don't she look like a witch, eh, on her ladder? Or a Jewess,
trussed on her tray for the boiler? *Her* turn now: where
others have gone, now she. What other people have, now
hers to suffer. Alone.

> *Leans stretcherhead on rostrumfoot, crouches on
> rostrum or ground, face close to hers. To us:*

Look, a tear. Swells up out of nothing in the socket of her
eye. The salt drop from the gland: fills, bulges, quivers.
Makes her look so stupid. You could want to smash her face
in, for looking so stupid. Weak face, stupid, helpless; slack
jaw, so helpless, stupid. It tears your heart in two for pity,
and your right hand itches up to strike that stupid face.
(Utterly straight, without pretence) There, dear, lie still. We'll
get your things together, don't you worry. *(To us again:)*
Beginning to shed; so shove her in gentle. *(Shoves stretcher
up along rostrum: into darkness)* Close the doors.

> *In apron still, Colin comes slowly; with deliberation
> clears potatoes, etc., then lounger away—they will
> not be needed now. On, off, on, off, unhurrying.
> While working so, to self:)*

Colin   *(quiet)* Now think. Think how this happens from some good
cause. If a bomb or a soldier had done it, you could be bitter.
Think, how it can have some—rightness. The way of nature.
Yet, was it in the way of nature, what we did? Lend her a
helping hand? Nature might—take unkindly to our—"help".
I rescued a shrew once, from the cat: yet the shrew ran
straight off the shovel, into a drain. The struggling in the
water; the sound of the little blind thing struggling in the
water. "Helped". It is true: what happens to us in the world,
bears no resemblance to "morality". Yet, from that—inequity,

might there not be a lesson to be learned ? We are so near the letters, how can we see the word ?

Silence.

In nature there is no annihilation. The dead are eaten. What remains rots down in corruption. In corruption itself murmur the bubbles of rebirth. Even what was burned, from ashes the fields are fertilized.
For all that : however a cosmos might absorb calamity, extinction's final—for the thing extinct.

> *Lightchange: Nurse comes, with white sheets, pillows, to transform rostrum to a hospital bed. Anne comes slowly (dazzling clean white nightdress), helped into bed, to lie facing us. Nurse raises Anne's head on pillows, continues off. Anne lies listless, telling us:*

Anne   We thought we'd saved it. The cervix contracted, it almost closed. One of the doctors, had hobnailed boots on his fingers : whenever he examined me— *(breath fails in remembered pain)* I'd only to *see* it was him on the wards, I'd start to bleed . . . But we thought we'd saved it. They even told Colin : "Come in with her clothes tomorrow, she'll be all right." But when he came, with the suitcase, "We're sorry," they said : "she's had a bad night; she must stay a while longer." One morning they rang him. "Your wife's going down to the theatre," they said. He saw what that meant. "I see," he said : "for the scrape, you mean." "Scrape ?" they said. "Well, if we've lost the baby—" he said. "Baby ?" they said : "What baby ?" They looked in the records : "It *is* Mr Harvey ?" "Harding," he said. "Oh. Harding. Oh no, Mr Harding, oh I *am* sorry, oh no, Mrs Harding's perfectly all right—". He was always last out of Visiting. One night, five minutes after he left, I wanted a crap. I called for the bedpan. But it wasn't a crap. It was just as easy as a crap. Easier. Plop, it was out— *(scream)* Nurse !

Darkness.

> *Bring up light, a blinding white: sheets, pillows behind Anne's head, a blinding white. Colin quietly comes, brings plain chair bedside, in his hand a pathetic bunch of fresh wild flowers he has picked for her, a share in the Spring she is missing:*

Colin   The ditches are white with stitchwort. *(Shows:)* Herb Robert. Cranesbill. Campion. *(Gives)*

Anne   *(no list to take them)* There were two. Two babies. One came, then I was unconscious; then the other, it woke me in the night. I said: Is it a boy? "Nothing," she said, "it's only clots." But it was a baby. I know it was. There were two. They were twins.

One must have gone wrong, you see. One must have been wrong from the start. So it died in the womb, it brought them both out, the good one with the bad. *(Motionless throughout)* The nurse won't tell me. I only want to know it wasn't a monster. Or that it *was* a monster. I don't know what it is I want to know. *(pause.)* They're in the fridge. They take them to the end of the ward and—put them in the fridge.

In the next ward you can hear the good ones crying, the ones that have been born. You have to have the different gyny wards together, that's only sense . . .

Colin   Next ward's where we'll be. Next time.

Anne   *(motionless, seems not to hear him)* I said to the doctor, I won't go through all this again. Oh, he's a patronizing bastard, the nurses queue up to kiss his arsehole—he's only a *doctor*! I won't go through this again, I told him: bugger this for a tale. Next time I start to bleed I'll go down to my husband's school and hire the trampoline.

Colin   Next time we'll be in there. This happens to one couple in five first time. We'll be in there next time.

Anne   *(utterly motionless. At last)* He said—he said—"There isn't going to be a next time, Mrs Harding. I'm sorry. We have had to take the womb away." *(pause)* "I'm sure your GP will recommend you for adoption."

> *Silence. Anne suddenly buries her head in Colin's breast:*

I'm sorry, love, I'm sorry—

Colin   *(stunned)* Why "sorry"—?

Anne   *(something indistinct) (i.e. About giving children—)*

Colin   *(can find nothing to say but)* No . . . No . . . *(i.e. Stop saying sorry)*

Anne   *(something indistinct) (i.e. About wanting to have* his *chil-dren—)*

Colin   No, no . . . Stop being so Arab. It's not "giving children", it's having. *Our* children, not mine. No. No.

Anne   *(constrained movement, orchestrating her pinned anguish)* I can see the smoke. From the incinerator. Burning my womb—!

> *They remain, motionless, silent. At last:*

Colin   *(very quiet)* Gone then. Gone. Gone. We must do what we can with what remains. All that, is gone.

Anne   *(utters one nigh-inaudible gasp of grief. Shakes bitterly, silent)*

Colin   *(deathly quiet)* Gone.

                    They remain so, motionless, silent. Then cut light.

III

*Chill pp music, spare, groping, desolate (Epilogue,
Vaughan Williams VI): in darkness strike stage bare;
two plain chairs only, now. Soon lifeless light: fade
music away. On chair sits Social Services Officer—
mid thirties, compassionate, quite smooth; suit clerical
grey, duplicated notes on crossed thighs. His chin
on a steeple of his hands, he eyes his audience, now
this couple, now that (who would be seated in a
nervous semicircle before him), perceivingly. Near
him, slightly upstage of and out of alignment with
him, seated on other chair: Area Adoptions Officer,
a woman in early thirties, smart, conventional, attrac-
tive; clipboard on lap. She would be discreetly
watching this couple, now that; noting a reaction
here, a giveaway gesture there; once or twice she
will, all but imperceptibly, make a brief mark on her
list of names, while Officer speaks:*

Officer   *(gentle, absolute, enshrining a hardness: he must prepare his
hearers for the worst)* We, in the Authority, realize you come
to us as a last resort. We accept that. You have discovered
for yourselves, there is no "host of unwanted children"
awaiting adoption: abortion laws, more tolerant attitudes to
illegitimacy, have seen to that. Private and religious agencies
are in abeyance; all over the country the lists are closing.
This application you have lodged with us is thus virtually
your last chance for parenthood of any kind. If then, as I
speak, you are furtively assessing these other couples'
chances with us as against your own, that is only under-
standable. For you know this is not a matter of rivalry
so much between you; yet you know also—if not, you are
not ready for adoption—to adopt means, not to find a child
you think suits *you*, but for us, the County, to find a home
we think right for the child. Thus, in the nature of things, we
can never say yes to you all. Even those of you, brave enough
to offer a home to a child of other or mixed race, or to a child
in some way handicapped, we shall almost always have to
turn away. There are not the children. Sad then though your
path has so far been, it may yet lead to further sadness. We
share that sadness. You come to adoption because you
have had to accept that natural parenthood is a common,
human, heritage from which you are shut out. You have

had to rethink parenthood; perforce matured, into seeing a possible child of yours, not as a product of your self, but as an infant person already possessed of his or her own history, bringing it with him, absolute in his own right. You have learned, a hard way, that in true parenthood there is no fantasy, no self-extension, no fond notion of vertical inheritance of what you think is best in *you*: you, leave such fatuous hopes behind, evolving perhaps toward something more like a parenthood of tomorrow. For some sociologists tell us, that tight little knot of domestic mirrors we call the Family, is a unit Man might now need to question and reject; that the family of tomorrow might possibly be something broader, more mixed—horizontal; fraternal. Many children, many parents, in one extended family. If so, then you, who have thought and fought your way through a peculiar disappointment and peculiar grief to some such— perhaps stand today more firmly on this threshold of tomorrow than those conventionally blest. But. If you have had cause for painful self-search before, I must warn you there is more to come. You would not feel safe in committing yourselves to a child of whom you knew nothing: still less can we hazard a child to a home of whose history values and likely future we had not found out all we reasonably could. You must be prepared, for prolonged and deep investigation: medical, professional, financial; marital. You will flinch from this inquisition; at times feel laid out on our slab just once too often. Appreciate our reasons. Nor is it pleasant for us, submitting a man's or a woman's deepest motives to dissection. Our Area Officer, Mrs Jones, who shares this casework, will endorse me on this.

> *Area Officer makes discreet minimal acknowledgement.*

Be warned. Expect little. Even if in the end we find you would make a most excellent couple for our list, it might still be most unlikely such a child will become available to us, as you will suit. In such a case, we prefer to get your disappointment over and done with straight away. Our reasons, however, for not accepting you, whatever they are, we never give. Painful though it is, to be found unsuitable and left wondering for ever why, we find that on balance it is safer for you, to be left in the dark. We marvel constantly at the courage would-be adoptive parents show. You begin to see now, how much you really need.

> *Light shrinks: Officer, Area Officer quietly go. From darkness, pale, naked but for pale-blue briefs, comes slowly Colin down to chair: in his hand, black leather shoes (in them, rolled-up socks), over his*

*arm a vest, white linen shirt, black tie, light cardigan
of fawn wool, black funeral suit.*

Colin   *(as he slowly dresses)* Last time I wore this, was over in
             Ireland too. Some country. Some "Mother". Only cause can
             bring us flying back till her is death . . . Poor Uncle Tommy.
             "Fine fella of a mahn." To end in pieces. What sort of son
             am I, to such fine fathers? White sterile son, dead branch of
             the tribe . . . No. No. All that's behind me. Progenitive
             fantasy, all behind me. For fatherhood I was not made.
             Nature was wise, she cast me from the start: dead seed,
             best fit to mix with excrement—ashes to ashes. *(sarcastic)*
             But I knew better. "I knowed better." I would be a "mahn".
             A "father". With cold water and bicarbonate of soda, chart
             calendar and clock—"Hi, oul' bitch, Nature!" I said, "I'll
             worst ye yet!" If I had been content—*(pauses)* Content . . .
             (sees truth of it) Content . . . my wife would have her womb
             this day. "Application for Adoption. Name, birthdate, address,
             profession, religion—none; average income, size of house,
             medical history—likelihood suddenly to die; biographical
             remarks—*(self-mocking)* I wrote them half a novel there . . .
             Two independent referees outside the family . . . First inter-
             view, the two of us, here. Next interview, there, myself
             alone: "Mr Harding, how genuinely motivated for parenthood
             do you think you are?"

             *He is dressed now. Sits on chair, black suit empha-
             sizing his pallor, his longing:*

             A child to come to us, absolute in his own right, his own
             inheritance, free of ours . . . Real child, a daughter, a son,
             real . . . Real flesh, real self, real person, real . . . to come to
             us, sidelong . . . Not down from us, but out, across the world,
             to us . . .

             *After a moment he goes up into darkness. Area
             Officer Mrs Jones comes with file, moves chair to
             a new position. Anne, pale, nervous, in drab camel
             coat, comes to sit in other chair, almost facing her.
             She takes off coat; her frock a bloodred shock, as
             though the blood on the tissue had grown through
             the stain on her nightdress to become all of her.
             Area Officer's tone throughout is utterly unrevealing,
             objective; quiet, compassionate, but searching. She
             hardly takes her eyes off Anne at all.*

Area Officer   Mrs Harding. How strongly do you want to become a parent?
Anne   I think our history answers that.
Area Officer   You have shown remarkable perseverance. When I spoke to

your husband, he said how much he admired your willpower
when you lay there—how did he put it?—"willing your foetus
to stay in place". I thought he, too, had from the beginning
shown quite frightening willpower. Why do you think he
did so?

Anne   For fatherhood.

Area Officer   Simply that?

Anne   *(thinking)* For Colin, fatherhood isn't a simple thing. Whenever I come to an interview I end up talking about him. It
was the same when I was trying for the stage: at auditions
we ended up talking about him. He used to write plays.

Area Officer   *(faintest wintry humour)* We talked about you last week.

Anne   Yes. When he got home I asked him how it went. "Lousy,"
he said, "I reckon I talked our child away."

Area Officer   *(silent. Then)* How do you think he would react, if we were
to turn down your application, knowing that with it there
almost certainly goes your last chance?

Anne   *(thinks. Then)* He'd be very bitter. Then he'd accept. What
else? We'd both accept. Then move on.

Area Officer   Away?

Anne   Oh no. I mean, if we're not to be parents, move on to what
we *can* become.

Area Officer   *(pause)* What do you think is your husband's worst fault?

Anne   Pigheadedness. It's a sort of—Protestant integrity, but it comes
over as pigheadedness.

Area Officer   When he discovered he had no future as a writer, he didn't
resist that. He turned away and started another life.

Anne   Thousands do that. I did that.

Area Officer   If we were to refuse you, what would your reaction be?

Anne   *(has pondered this already)* It would all seem part of the—
evolving pattern.

Sees Area Officer would like her to amplify.

When our careers collapsed, his and mine, we began to read
it as a sort of message, if you like: that we ought to—take a
different road. We came out here; we went back to teaching,
for which we'd both been trained; we became rural and
domestic. Soon the idea of children became important. Well,
you know what happened about *that*. So. If we're turned
down, it'll be pretty conclusive this was a wrong road, too.

Long silence.

Area Officer   How strong do you think your marriage is?

Anne thinks.

	What do you think is the greatest threat to it?
Anne	*(at last)* If one knew *that* . . .

Area Officer Your husband's answer to this question was: *(Brief glance at notes)* "When the earthquake happens, the buildings that survive are the ones that swayed." How do you think he means, your marriage could sway? His rather unorthodox sexuality, you think because of that?

Anne I don't think he meant the *marriage* could sway. I think he meant about people rolling with the punches that Nature gives them.

Area Officer Yet you say he is pigheaded.

Anne *(candid)* He's learning.

Pause.

Anyway. I don't think his sexuality is unorthodox. His acknowledgement of it might be. We have to tell you these things.

Area Officer That he can consciously feel for his own sex, do you think that threatens your marriage?

Anne I feel safer.

Area Officer Safer?

Anne Safer than if he had a roving eye for other women. Anyway, I've told him: if he has to have a bit of the other sex once in a while, just be sure to come back clean. It's how he's made; he has only one life. Likewise me. If I *have* to succumb to the milkman, he says "Just not in *our* bed". It's a joke but . . . a grain of truth. If that shocks you, I'm sorry.

Area Officer It doesn't *shock* me—

Anne We don't abuse each other's liberality. Anyway, men with open homosexual emotions are supposed to make good fathers. It's just a rotten consequence of natural logic so few of them get the chance.

Area Officer Is your marriage satisfactory, Mrs Harding?

Anne Bed, you mean?

Area Officer Among other things.

Anne Not always. In fact, it's rather bad just now. The tension all this has put us under. And the fact that I shall never conceive does—to begin with, anyway—make some difference. He's not the great greasy bullock of my dreams, what woman's husband is? It's probably better to find your man tolerable company for fifty years than be hooked on his cock. I don't even like my husband all the time: but for good or ill he's in my belly now.

Area Officer *(at last)* What do you think you have to offer a child, Mrs Harding?

Anne   *(thinks a long time. Then)* Nothing. Specific. Just what we'd
        have to offer children of our own. I can't think of anything.
        Just a—share in living.

> *Cut light. Already we can hear airport-sound, loud
> aircraft landing. In darkness strike all, bring bare
> rostrum mid-centre, set chairs as front seats in a
> van. Ding-dong, voice of airport announceress:
> "BEA announce the arrival of flight number BE four-
> two-five from Belfast." Repeat. Sounds of airport
> corridor, many people trooping. Fade aircraft sounds.
> Two car doors slam; sound of ignition, car pulling
> away. Up faintest light. Colin, Anne sit as in van, he
> passenger in coat, she by implication driving.*

Colin   *(trying for thousandth time to realify the horror to himself)*
        They all stood, paralyzed. Someone had said "There's a
        second bomb, keep away". But after a minute they could
        bear the tension no longer; they all rushed forward. In.
        They say the scene that met their eyes was—unspeakable.
        Pieces of people, hunks of unrecognizable torn flesh;
        pathetic items of shopping, clothes, schoolbooks; a boy's
        head. The nethers of a pregnant woman, skewered on a bus-
        stop shaft. Spatters of digest, shite and half-shite. Tissue,
        bone, deep slimes of blood; a knot of intestines slowly slid-
        ing down a wall. Atrocious anagram of people going home.
        A Swedish photographer, had Auschwitz Korea the Congo
        Vietnam in his belt, had to be carried away hysterical and
        vomiting. Somewhere in that, Uncle Tommy had died. To
        that conclusion, his days had been bringing him all along.
        What call have we, to be appalled? What claim have we,
        on moral repugnance? What's so especially obscene about
        this sort of bomb? That it comes from below? Delivered by
        citizen to fellow-citizen, not sent long-distance through the
        air above? Local, and small enough, to class as an outrage:
        not global, and technocratic enough, to rank as policy?
        Just ends do not justify violent means, we are told. Except
        of course on a governmental scale. Ireland as ever brings
        that logic remorselessly home where it belongs. To us. And
        here, by God, only beginneth the lesson. "So why did ye
        stay across the water so long?" Aunt Annie said. "Ye know
        ye could have come live wi' us at any time, why did ye not
        come here?" she said: "wi' us?" I said: Because I was
        afeared. Truth to tell, Aunt Annie, I was afeared to come.
        Forbye, because I am so torn. "Between what?" Between the
        baker's halfdozen wrongs of this all. Torn, I tried to tell her,
        torn wondering where best—no, not where best; where at
        all we go now. "Aunt Annie"—my heart was in my mouth

as I said it—"we've known from Year One our old North of Ireland had to go some time." As a child,* every August the Twelfth, I marched with the Prentice Boys round Derry Walls. The Fenians* in Bogside would save their filthiest rubbish to burn that day, so the smoke from their chimneys'd dirty our shirts. And I really believed: that, was a moral disposition of the world. Oh, this side the water I might wonder, a little, what life was like below those walls—and there are Bogsides here, too. I have always known trouble would come in that city. When the riots broke out, I was disturbed: I began to wonder. Awful to say, but only these bombs have made me really think. If an undertribe can commit themselves to such atrocity, there must be some terrible misery they are trying to communicate. And our . . . *(Searches self deeply for these words:)* inequity . . . monopoly of things . . . self— . . . *(This last word he almost fails to find. Self-satisfaction, no. Tries again)* Self— . . . *(Still cannot find. At long last, after appalling self-search)* —certainty . . . *(Pause)* Self-certainty and acquiescence . . . add up to a muckheap only violence will shift. Sure, we've known all along our old ways had to go. Some time. The reckoning come. Some time. The whirlwind. In someone's time. The whirlwind is here. In our time.— All that is gone, Aunt Annie, I said: all we depended on for our identity has gone, ourselves have helped to pull it down. Not all the commissions corporations facelifts in the world can make that stand again. Our only hope: did the seed of anything good come out? What—new people we have it in us to become. "We, is it, now?" she says; "*we* is it? An' you safe in Englan' all this time."

We went into the room at the back where—what is left of Lily Martin lives. Aunt Annie had tried to prepare me: "You not show your shock, now." I clapped eyes on—that trunk of her, no legs, no arms; the head bald as an egg, half the features blown away. The breath was dashed out of me, I had no breath left to try to—hide my horror. And Lily saw. Three hours out of the twenty-four she'll sleep now; the other twenty-one she cries. Cousin Sammy came, was, and is, to marry her. He stood beneath the picture of the Duke of Edinburgh and the Queen: in his anorak, cap, dark glasses; with his stick. "It's well for you," he said, "across the water. We here have to fight. To save the land we love." I wanted to say There are other ways to fight. I wanted to say This way of yours, what shall you do to this "land you love"? I wanted to say Do I not love this land as well as you?—I've only to think of the Nine Glens; Lough Fea* on Slieve G— . . . *(But the mountain's name itself he suddenly represses:)* Sentiment. Think of Bogside; Burntollet; the rot-

* See Appendix.

ten *wrongness* there has been, the wrongness I in my own
acquiescence have been a part of . . . I love that land; her
I carry . . . But . . . Violence will never pay, we are told.
But it does; and in our hearts we know it does. I: have been
part of a muck that only violence *can* shift. Yet I said to
Sam "Soon or late, this violence must end. Sooner or
later, the bloodshed has to stop: can't the lesson be drawn
from it now?" I didn't put what I said so bravely nor so
well. I was frightened. I had to—choose my words. "I
just think," I said, "I just think we have to try to find some
new way, up, out of this, Sammy," I tried to say, "we have
been a great people. Twice in history our Protestant ex-
istence here has turned a tide of tyranny back: once, against
the Catholic monarchies of Europe; more recently, deny-
ing Hitler the freedom of the ocean—moments not to be
underestimated nor forgotten. Now we are on the anvil
a third time. Can we rise to the occasion this third time,
then? Turn a third tyranny back? The tyranny of our own—
(Now it hits Colin, and the clarity of it is freeing him:)
inheritance? Our inheritance *is* glorious: but all that has to
be behind us now. Shed. I just—I just think we just have to—
try to see, what new selves we can rise up out of this, and
become. Oh Sammy, if we can do that, oh then we are a
brave tribe." *(Perhaps with a hint of Sammy's up-you gesture:)*
"Phoenix yerself." Uncle Tommy's coffin lay in the front par-
lour of the house, for friends and neighbours to come filing
in and see: "Lord bless us but he makes a lovely corpse." Only
Tommy's coffin was closed. Tommy's was closed. One of the
neighbour-women even said: "Your Tommy was a large
mahn. His coffin is so small." In the morning, the men all came
to carry him to his grave. I went to put my shoulder to the coffin
to do my share of the bearing. The men pushed me aside.
And Sam said *(Quiet, reasonable:)* "You'll carry no Ulster-
man's coffin to no grave. Stay here wi' the weemen." The
drum beat. Up the street, to the Orange Hall then to the
grave, went with that coffin all my—belonging . . . The
women did not speak to me. I felt so severed. *(No self-pity,
but an absolute new clear-seeing:)* I know it is the strongest
feeling in the world, to be alone. And I did feel strong. Yet,
the land, from whose earth I belong, the clan, from whose
loins I come, had turned me out; to my own loins no child
of tomorrow shall come: and I felt so— *(At last)* severed.

> *Long silence: he takes out, lights, a cigarette (only
> time anyone smokes in entire play). Peers out of
> sidewindow into dark. For him, though a sorrow, it
> is also a setting free:*

So. There's another—"self" for the rubbish heap with all

the rest. My self as "tribal son". Yet: if we do not change, tomorrow has no place for us.

> *Cut light. On speakers: wide-spaced piano-arpeggi, in slow five-finger groups, stepwise haltingly ascend, descend in C major, C minor, A flat major; D flat, etc. Strike chairs. Slow fade up cold light: a wheelbarrow with newdug potatoes, Anne in rough coat seated on rostrumfoot carefully sorting—those cut or speared in digging, into a box or basket, for immediate use; the good, gently into a bulging half-hundredweight paper sack; the blighted, on to a spread local newspaper, for discarding.*

Anne

Bloody piano. "Exercise to stretch the webs between the fingers." Why won't he *accept* his hands are too small? In winter his skin hardens, the webs split and bleed. I begin to wonder: does he only try at what he knows he can't achieve? Some sort of escape, that. Lord grant me learn my proper parish . . .

> *Fade piano out meanwhile. A blighted potato breaks between Anne's finger and thumb:*

Irishman, and these he grows. *(puts it on to paper)* Still . . . Blight. Good years and bad. Luck . . . Husbandry . . . I could gorge between my legs now the milk of a thousand men and it all perish, safe. Stop; stop. Burn these. *(An advert in the paper catches her eye:)* "What is it makes the Arnolds so full of beans?" *(Wry, resuming work)* What *is* it, makes the Arnolds so full of beans?

> *Becomes conscious of a sound we do not hear (electric sawing in distance):*

Elms being felled . . .* All the parks, fields, farms of the county, elms being felled. Bark stripped off and burnt, roots ripped up and burnt. Along the roads their tall crowns wither, grow bald, their doomed stems marked with a white painted cross. And the farmers burn the stubble all over, day and night—when by law they should not—to burn the wheat-rust out. And because it's cheaper. Singe the orchards, burn the hedgerows with their buds and berries down, because it's cheaper. Pillage the earth, and before it's rested, radge it with a winter crop. Squeeze the earth dry, she'll last just about as long as we shall; bugger our sons.

> *Elsewhere, another sound we do not hear:*

* See Appendix.

Jeff Walton, altering his pigs he's bought. They grub their
own testicles up from the ground where they've fallen, and
eat them. I just remember my dream. I was teaching the children. Suddenly I said "Oh children, all you children, go under,
all go under, quickly, quickly." Outside it was bright blue day.
Such blue. Suddenly I saw in the sky huge vessels, shaped
like the upturned abdomens of wasps, striped yellow-and-
red, yellow-and-green, upcurling and vanishing into the
blue. I knew what they were. The air was clammy with a
fine invisible mist, in the sunshine all the people shopping
had begun to vomit and spit. I ran to the chemist's for a
sink to puke in but his door was padlocked. In all the
house-windows, notices: Clean Water Five pee. I came
home. I said, "Colin, I did what I could, I brought home
what I could." But in my basket there was nothing. I cried
at that. I cried such tears, the wild upwelling that we weep
in dreams. He was trying to make love to me. His penis
was arid and red hot. I was pretending. Suddenly he screamed
and leapt away from me, bent over. "Oh, what's the matter,
my love?" I said; "tell me the matter." He said—when the
seed came out of him, it was scalding spit, it tore out of
his knob like the E string of a violin—and I saw: it had ripped
up and back along his shaft like a cheesewire. I touched
him: I wanted to make him better, I touched him, his flesh
turned hard, then scaly like a fish. I could see he was dying.
He was—dying—Then he was dead. I came out across the
marsh. The sky was red like blood. The land was black.
The cabbages had been blasted from their stalks, the stalks
stood gnarled and knotted in rows, unnaturally gleaming. I
was weak. I could see my body was turning scaly as his
had done. I dragged myself to where I could lean against
a thorntree. I lay there. A child came. No child that I would
call a child. A child of ice, moving without seeming to
move, crossing the black flat of the marsh beneath the red
sky. He-she-it, featureless, white, its head in a dome like
a child from space. I was so frightened, so weak I could
not lift myself at all; I felt I was going out, like water down
a drain: into extinction . . . *(Thinks, does not say: "But no
. . ." New tone, of coming resurrection:)* I woke. A voice
overlapped from the dream: the child's and mine: the same.
"Take *off* your dead" . . .

> *Quietly Colin comes, in anorak, cords again; opened
> letter in hand.*

Colin   *(terse)* From the County. *(Face, voice show nothing)*

> *Anne snatches letter, glancing at his face; then
> reads. Colin leans arms upon rostrumside, reading*

> paper without taking any of it in; a covert glance at
> Anne. She is looking up, forward, out, letter in
> hand on lap. Colin waits till it is time for him to
> speak:

(Not cold; but inly stricken of all expression) That's it.
Another "us" to shed: mummy and daddy. (Looks down
at paper again. Eye catches something. With tiniest chuckle:)
"Day-old boy found in lavatory pan in Worcester." The world
is like this.

> Anne says nothing. Colin does not look up.

(A there-it-is tone) Laughter of children in our house, not
for us. Whatever is.

> Yes. Whatever is. This road must now be abandoned
> also. Anne sees it; inly she has known it all along. It is
> pitiful, but they are released. Their hopes for parent-
> hood lie in ashes, but on some other road must lie
> whatever is for them. After a moment she turns her-
> self, without standing, toward Colin; and now he
> must learn to look at her, frank in his inadequacies, his
> reality, just as he is, all male personae shed.

> A Beginning.

APPENDIX

p. 26   Delius.

In fact, a traditional (Lincolnshire) melody. The actor must take care that the B is natural throughout; especially at the end of bar 2 there will be a tendency to pitch it flat.

p. 28   "Primate" should strictly be "primip" for "primipara" — bearing for the first time. The mishearing is originally mine or my wife's; so it could equally plausibly be Anne's. It would not be a good moment for a doctor to correct her.

p. 29   Blankets, sheets, etc., are better referred to as "bedclothes" if, as is more theatrically practicable, a continental quilt is used; in which case, Anne should perhaps say "It'll come through to the mattress", she can't "lie on a wet mattress".

p. 30   For some reason, audiences tend to laugh at this: perhaps they hear "goldfish". (On a similar point of acoustic clarity, the Guru should be careful on p. 18 that the audience do not mishear his "sufficiency" as "efficiency", there being an s-sound immediately before it.)

p. 47   Some members of an audience can still (believe it or not) be in doubt as to Colin's religious-cultural allegiances even as late in the play as this: so, except obviously in Ireland or with Irish audiences, he should perhaps here say "As a good Protestant child . . ." and speak of the "Catholics" in Bogside. Irish audiences might notice one or two minor inauthenticities in Colin's usage: but these reflect either his Protestant unfamiliarity with Catholic idiom (e.g. his "Bogside" for their "The Bogside"—the use of the defnite article with certain placenames is a real shibboleth in Ulster) ; or his already advanced separateness from Ulster itself.

p. 47   Lough Fea—pronounced, roughly, "fey"—is a very lonely and haunted-seeming lough high up on Slieve Gallion in mid-Tyrone. (On a possibly relevant personal note, I remember that it was by the side of this lough one cold autumn day that, as a student, I heard the news that Sibelius had died.)

For better clarity, with non-Irish audiences, Burntollet should perhaps be referred to as "the ambush at Burntollet"—where Civil Rights marchers on their way to Derry were set upon by "Protestants" armed with bottles and stones and sticks with nails: one of the incidents (January 1969) that helped precipitate the present conflict.

p. 49   The exercise is one of my own, an application of the Beringer study-principle, for increasing the pliability of the hands in dense chord-formation:

—a seven-group span, doubled (here) in the bass at two octaves' distance. Second time through, play every E as E♭; third time, replace the G also, with an A♭: the arpeggio thus modulates from C major through C minor to A♭ major. The process can then be repeated from D♭ major, and so on . . . But in the theatre we should begin to lose this sound-effect once the first change of harmony has taken place.

p. 49   It is possible that where Dutch Elm Disease is not known of, or the 1970s epidemic of it in midland and southern England is forgotten, the line should read "Sick elms being felled."